PREFACE

The purpose of the *Hobart Papers* is to contribute a series of authoritative, independent and lucid economic commentary to the study of industrial and public policy. The characteristic concern is the optimum use of scarce resources in response to consumer preferences within a legal and institutional framework governing the ownership of property and the conduct of contract.

One of the essential parts of the framework is the environment within which industry can most effectively serve society by responding to consumer preferences. Since 1890 the USA has developed a structure of anti-trust ('trust-busting') laws. Although imperfect and sometimes lagging behind technical development, it has helped to maintain a generally competitive economy. In Britain, the development of anti-trust laws is more recent, but since 1948 a series of measures directed against monopoly and restrictive practices has created the substance of British 'trust-busting'.

The structure of industry is thus the result of two sets of elements: the economic and the legal. Economies of scale in technique, management, marketing, financing and risk-taking tend to increase the size and reduce the number of units of control, known as 'firms': diseconomies tend to reduce the size and increase the number. But at a given point in time, or in a given period, the structure of industry is also the outcome of the legal and institutional framework that permits or even encourages the development of firms that are larger (or, less frequently, smaller) than their optimum economic size.

In recent years the British economy has seen the emergence of mergers not only between firms that seem natural complements to one another in horizontal or vertical integration but also 'conglomerates' that seem to have no evident common identity. In Hobart Paper No. 1 Professor B. S. Yamey of the London School of Economics analysed the practice of resale price maintenance; in No. 3 Mr Anthony Vice examined the 'take-over' convulsion of the late 1950s; in No. 11 Mr John Heath considered the measures desirable to increase competition; and in No. 37

Dr F. R. Jervis argued that some firms had expanded by 'diversification' without adding significantly to efficiency and often in opposition to the interests of shareholders. Mr Guy Naylor in No. 7 and Professor Harold Rose in Eaton Paper No. 1 also argued, from different approaches, that the British law governing the formation and conduct of companies was inadequate to ensure the most efficient use of shareholders' money. In Research Monograph No. 5 Dr Mario Deaglio discussed the Italian Istituto per la Ricostruzione Industriale at a time when the Industrial Reorganisation Corporation (IRC) was being formed in Britain with much the same purpose of encouraging industrial mergers.

Ten years after the first *Hobart Paper*, Dr Brian Hindley, also of the London School of Economics, turns to an analysis of possible structural imperfections in British industry and what seems to be government policy desirable to ensure that it serves the general interest of the consumer by maximising economies and minimising costs. His *Paper* comes at the point when IRC has spent several years and large sums of public money encouraging mergers it considered desirable and preventing others it considered undesirable. Dr Hindley examines the *rationale* for its activities by discussing the reasons why firms merge with one another and asks why their judgement should be thought inferior to the judgement of an outside body such as the IRC. As a major reason for doubting whether mergers between firms serve the consumer, he discusses possible divergences between the interests of owners and managers. He contends that researches do not provide sufficient support for government-sponsored activities such as those of the IRC, but concludes that the possibility of conflict between managerial decisions and the interests of owners and the general public remains.

It does not follow from this, he argues, that a panoply of official bodies should be established, each with its area of discretion, often conflicting with that of another. The problem could better be dealt with by removing the market imperfections that give rise to it. This solution would require an environment in which the threat of take-over to a slack management was substantially increased.

[4]

Such an approach could mean an increase in merger activity. It is difficult to know how the government would react to any one merger—even more to a number. Dr Hindley therefore examines the criteria by which mergers should be judged. He concludes, first, that the government should ban concentration-increasing mergers between firms in the same activity, subject to an appeal at which firms would be required to demonstrate potential economies of scale in order that the ban should be removed; second, that it should allow other types of mergers to proceed unchecked.

It might be added that if government builds a structure of agencies with administrative discretion, such as the IRC, on the plausible ground that 'something must be done' because in practice the market is imperfect, the urgency and the urge to perfect it would be weakened or destroyed.

Dr Hindley believes that much of government policy towards industry is based on the supposition that managers can act at variance with the interests of owners. But he does not think that this is a sufficient justification for that policy. He concludes that better reasons are required if government policy towards industry is to continue in its present forms.

The Institute is grateful to Professor S. R. Dennison, who has made studies of the structure of industry, and to Sir Arnold Plant, a former member of the Monopolies Commission, for reading an early draft of Dr Hindley's paper and offering comments and suggestions. Like them, and the members of its Advisory Council, the Institute does not necessarily share Dr Hindley's analysis or conclusions, but offers his *Paper* as an authoritative, closely-reasoned and concentrated analysis of development in British industry and of government policy for students and teachers of economics, for business men whose confidence in their capacity to take decisions may have been weakened in recent years, and for politicians of all parties and especially in the incoming Government who are to 'drastically modify' the IRC Act.[1]

June 1970   EDITOR

[1] *A Better Tomorrow*, Conservative Party Manifesto, 1970, Conservative Central Office.

CONTENTS

THE AUTHOR

BRIAN HINDLEY went to school at Queen Elizabeth's Grammar School, Mansfield, Notts. He emigrated to Canada shortly after completing National Service (RAF), and entered the University of Chicago in 1958. He became a member of Phi Beta Kappa on the award of a BA, and obtained a doctorate from Chicago in 1967. While completing the research for a PhD thesis he lectured at Queen's University, Ontario, Canada. He joined the London School of Economics in 1967 as a Lecturer in Economics.

I. INTRODUCTION

In recent years there has been a distinct tendency for government policy towards business to be based on the idea that firms do not, or at least might not, attempt to maximise the earnings on the investment of their owners. The truth of this proposition is not self-evident; and if it were widely accepted, it would imply a different relationship between government and business from the one that has obtained in the past.

The Government is now in different hands, and there is little doubt that policy will change. But the presumptions and attitudes which led to the policy of the previous administration are still present, and the change of government does not alter the nature of the underlying problem which must be considered when industrial policy is formulated. The problem and its implications will be discussed in the following pages; but first, consider some illustrations of this tendency drawn from the area of government policy towards mergers between business firms.

Government approach to mergers

The Board of Trade pamphlet *Mergers*[1] lists 116 questions which the Board's merger panel 'may' ask about mergers which come before it for review. Among them are the following:

'Para. 39(2) What are the management prospects? How far is the overall level of management likely to be raised: What prospects are there in fact of synergy between the two firms (i.e. that the merged group can achieve a more effective use of resources than the two companies separately)? What assessment can be made of the quality of the existing management? What plans are there for reorganisation of the management of the new group? Who will in fact be responsible for carrying the merger through?'

[1] Board of Trade, *Mergers: A Guide to Board of Trade Practice*, HMSO, 1969.

Or, in the section dealing with conglomerate merger:

'Para. 58(3) What is likely to be the effect of the merger on the efficiency of the different sectors of production of the existing conglomerate or the acquired company? What is the management structure of the conglomerate? Is performance between different sectors uneven? Is the range of industries included too wide for effective and progressive over-all management? Is there extensive cross-subsidisation between the different industrial sectors, with the more successful supporting the continuation of less efficient sectors?'

And:

'What are the future management plans for the new group? Compatibility of management of the acquiring and acquired firm? Will there be an undue concentration in the new group of managerial decision-making?'

Clearly, these questions raise issues which are of direct interest to the owners of firms. Any answer which the Board would find unpalatable on behalf of the public interest would also be unpalatable for the owners in their private interest. That the Board nevertheless finds it necessary to ask them suggests either that it believes that owners are too foolish to recognise their interest or answer these questions as competently as can the Board, or that firms may not be operated in the interests of their owners.

The Board's merger panel decides whether a merger should be referred to the Monopolies Commission, and if it refers a conglomerate merger[1] the Commission will ask the same kinds of question. In the appendix to its report on the Rank-De La Rue merger proposal, the Commission argues that economies of scale which may result from horizontal and vertical mergers may be sufficient to offset losses resulting from the impairment to competition. It continues:

[1] A conglomerate merger is one in which there is no common product in the activities of the merging firms. A merger between two firms engaged in the same activity would be horizontal, while one between firms at different stages in the same production process would be defined as vertical. Thus, for example, a merger between two firms engaged in the production of television sets would be classified as horizontal; one between a television set manufacturer and a tube maker as vertical; and the purchase by a meat packer of a firm at any stage in television set production as conglomerate.

'Conversely, in conglomerate mergers, losses in efficiency may in some cases be found sufficiently likely and substantial, even in the absence of anti-competitive consequences, to cause the merger to be regarded as contrary to the public interest. It is proper that in both cases the efficiency with which the country's resources are likely to be used should be considered.'[1]

In this context, efficiency means using the smallest quantity of resources compatible with a given output: it is not clear why the Commission cannot leave that aspect of a merger to the owners of the firms who are, after all, the people who pay for the resources their firm uses and who presumably do not want to pay more than they must.[2]

On the more positive side of government policy, the Industrial Reorganisation Corporation (IRC) was established with the primary purpose of paying firms to merge with one another in order to achieve, *inter alia*, the supposed benefits of economies of scale. But if there are indeed economies of scale, the joint profits of the two firms would be higher if they pooled their resources. If they will not merge unless they are offered special inducements to do so, they cannot be obtaining the largest possible returns for their owners. The existence of the IRC must therefore be predicated on the belief that firms will not be operated in their owners' interests.

One could multiply examples. But these will suffice to demonstrate the kind of policy with which this *Paper* is concerned.

The burden of the loss from poor decisions

It should be said immediately that the decision of two firms to merge or not to merge may prove in the event to have been mistaken. Any decision regarding the future may be wrong; some decisions will be wrong; and wrong decisions are costly in resources. But the crucial point in all of these cases is the *incidence* of the waste of resources resulting from the incorrect decision.

---

[1] Reprinted in *Mergers, ibid.*, pp. 40–49.
[2] Nor is it clear why the Commission restricts its comments to conglomerate merger. It is conceivable that firms which restrict their merger activity to technically related industries could also become too large for efficient operation; if the Commission thinks it proper to speculate on future efficiency in the one case, why not in the other?

Consider, for example, a conglomerate merger in which a chalk maker buys a cheese manufacturer. Suppose the chalk maker's decision is bad, and his acquisition turns out to be unprofitable: he expected to reduce the costs of output of the cheese firm but he finds that they increase as a result of his management. The increase in costs is a loss from society's point of view: it represents additional resources used up in the production of cheese which could have been used in producing other commodities (or services). But the person who suffers the loss is the owner of the chalk firm. The rest of the community can use as many resources as it otherwise would have done. The additional resources used in the production of cheese are matched by a reduction in the chalk maker's income: income that would have been spent in using resources for his consumption if he had not used it—willy-nilly—buying the additional resources used wastefully to produce cheese. The same analysis applies to two firms which could have achieved additional economies of scale if they had merged but decide, for whatever reason, not to do so. Their output could have been produced at a lower cost in resources, and to that extent, society loses by their decision. But the 'social' loss appears as a reduction of the income of the owners of the two firms who took the wrong decisions to below that which they could have enjoyed had they merged their firms.

A part of the losses might be shifted to the rest of the community. The most obvious and direct way is that if profits are reduced the government, which shares in profits by taxation, will lose revenue. This means that either government services must be reduced or that taxes must be increased elsewhere, and either of these possibilities could result in losses for others than the owners.[1] A more subtle loss occurs if the increase in the costs of an acquired firm can be offset by an increase in prices. This would occur if it possessed some monopoly power. Again, if poor merger decisions were frequent, the risk involved in holding wealth in the form of shares might be increased, and the allocation of capital worsened.

[1] I do not know whether anyone would consider this a sufficient ground for intervention in private decision-making. If so, they would presumably extend the principle to a worker who chooses not to work overtime, thereby depriving the rest of us of the income tax on the foregone earnings, or to a housewife who buys untaxed rather than taxed goods. The applications are endless, *ad absurdum*.

These possibilities are inherent in all business decisions, not only those which take the form of a merger. But they should not obscure the more important consideration that the private interest of the owners of the acquiring firm, or of the firm which decides not to acquire another, is so large that one would not expect them to make a habit of rash or ill-considered decisions. Since there is no doubt that incorrect decisions will be made from time to time, it is quite possible that a check on mergers would prevent some which would have been failures, and that a body to encourage mergers might induce some which are successful; but since there is also no doubt that the official body would not itself be infallible, it is also quite possible—and, since it does not have the same direct interest, more likely—that it would prevent some mergers which would have proved to be to the public benefit, and would induce some which are against it.

Conflict between public and private interests

To argue thus is not to argue that firms should be left to their own devices. The proper relationship between government and business has always been, and will continue to be, a vexed topic. Nevertheless, there is a minimum level of agreement: nobody would now argue that there are no possible conflicts between the interests of the owners of firms and of the community at large and that, if firms were left to do as they pleased subject only to the constraints of private property rights, the outcome would not be an optimum allocation of resources. In other words, this policy would not produce an allocation such that it would be impossible to make one person better off without making another worse off.

There are two reasons why even those who favour *laissez-faire* policies would (or should) agree that the policies they advocate would produce a sub-optimal allocation of resources.[1] First, firms

---

[1] Agreement that minimal government intervention would produce a sub-optimal allocation of resources does not, in logic, destroy the case for *laissez-faire* policies. However, advocacy of such policies must then rest upon the lack of efficacy of corrective governmental policies. (By *laissez-faire* I mean broadly a system in which government is limited to establishing and enforcing exclusive private property rights where that is feasible; and of undertaking any further role in economic activity only where they are not feasible—for example, national defence.)

may have some degree of monopoly power, and managers concerned to maximise returns to the owners would then have an incentive to charge a higher price, and produce less, than would be best from the point of view of the community as a whole.

Second, firms might use methods of production which give rise to costs for the rest of the community but do not appear as costs to the firm. This is the problem of 'externality'; the traditional text-book example is that of a firm which, in its efforts to produce at least cost, uses production methods that create large amounts of smoke. The smoke makes life unpleasant for people in its vicinity; but if they have no means of charging the firm for this pollution, it has no pecuniary incentive to change to a method of production creating less smoke. There are many similar examples: one of contemporary interest is firms which do not avoid polluting water because they are not charged for the harm they cause to other water users.

But the import of these cases should not be mistaken. Given the correct institutional framework, it is desirable that firms should strive to maximise profits. This must then mean that they are attempting to supply the goods buyers want while minimising the costs of their chosen level of output, thus leaving as much as possible of society's scarce resources for the production of other things. When monopoly or externality is present, the attempt to maximise profits, while still laudable as a managerial characteristic, no longer means that the managers' actions are the best possible for the community as a whole. There is a conflict between private and public interests.

In such circumstances governmental action can readily be justified. But the type of policy to be discussed in this *Paper* involves no such conflict: the interests of the owners of firms in maximising returns to themselves will, if translated into action, produce exactly the results which the government finds it necessary to check or to encourage. It is this which gives rise to doubts about the appropriateness of governmental action.

A further consideration is of wider significance. Much of the centuries-old debate on normative economics concerns the extent to which social decision-making can be decentralised without incurring economic losses. The market, on this view, is not only an efficient means of making necessary choices, but simultaneously also a device by which they can be made outside the political process. The issues of centralisation *versus* de-centralisation cannot properly be treated in this *Paper;* I must assume that at least some of my readers are persuaded of the virtues of de-centralised choice where it is possible.

From this aspect, the contention that private business cannot be relied upon to ensure that resources are efficiently used and that the government or its agencies must step in to provide that assurance is significant since it requires a further centralisation of decision-making and the grant of broad discretionary power to officials who oversee the operation of the policies.

Discretionary power is generally objectionable since it can be used for other purposes than visualised by the politicians who granted it: for personal aggrandisement; for the expression of the personal prejudices of officials to whom it was granted; or as a means of compelling the people against whom it was granted to do things quite different from those intended by the legislators. In addition, its appropriate use may require specialised knowledge, so that with the best will in the world officials who must use it are unlikely to do so in a way which produces the desired outcome; while in its nature it adds an element of uncertainty to the planning of business men against whom it can be applied.

These arguments are applicable to the discretionary powers granted to the government and its agencies in their relations with private business; but they do not mean, in that case or any other, that discretionary powers should never be granted to official bodies. The point is rather that their grant should be conditional upon the demonstration of some clear and probable gain.

Prima facie, the kind of policy to be considered has little to recommend it. It substitutes official action where the private interests of the owners of firms might be expected to produce the desired results; it does so in decisions where they are the principal losers if errors are made and the principal gainers if they are corrected; and it can work only through the grant of wide discretionary power to official bodies. It seems inconceivable that better uses cannot be found for governmental resources.

II. POSSIBLE JUSTIFICATIONS FOR OFFICIAL INTERVENTION

The belief that civil servants and members of government-created bodies can usefully intervene in business decisions when there is no conflict between the interests of the community and those of the owners could, in principle, be defended on several grounds; but it is difficult to identify any one of these as *the* official view. Speeches by relevant members of the government make frequent references to '. . . poor and out-of-date management in British industry',[1] and it has become an official truism that 'At the root of much of what is wrong in British industry lies an ingrained resistance to change—both in the boardroom and on the shop floor'.[2] One sees behind such comments the vision of a Britain made great by the transference of dynamic Whitehall attitudes to the sleepy private sector; but they beg the question at issue. Why is it not possible to rely on *owners* to dispose of the incompetent managers who burden them?

Business decision-making: does Whitehall know best?

The most obvious answer is that the managers and owners of firms do not recognise their interests as clearly as do those with official status, or that they are less capable of seeing the best way to realise them. Conversation with any civil servant concerned with the regulation of industry here or in the United States will produce putative instances of civil service ability to make more profitable decisions than those made by the business men involved. There is no reason to doubt the accuracy of many of these assertions: business men do make mistakes, and civil servants are not stupid. But this is not a sufficient basis for a persuasive

---

[1] From a speech of the President of the Board of Trade (then Mr Anthony Crosland), reprinted in *Mergers, op. cit.*, p. 58.
[2] Industrial Reorganisation Corporation, *Report 1968/69*, p. 20.

argument that the decisions of civil servants or of official bodies should be enforced. Whitehall officials or appointees have neither the same *knowledge* of a business nor the same direct *incentive* to make profitable decisions as the business men running it. There is no reason to suppose that official decisions on a business would in general be superior to those of its managers; and a good deal of reason to suppose that they would be inferior. It is difficult to conceive of a valid argument for intervention in business decisions based upon this rather arrogant assertion; though, in practice, it may be self-fulfilling. Is it likely that a society in which it is assumed that government appointees or civil servants are more competent to take business decisions than the managers will succeed in establishing or maintaining a thriving industrial machine?

Official bodies may possess information which is relevant to a business decision but which is not available to the business men responsible for making it. The mere possession of information by officials, however, is not sufficient to make a case for transferring the decision to their hands or giving them a right to change it; it must also be shown that the information cannot be given to private decision-makers so that their choices are not biased through lack of available and relevant knowledge. It is difficult to believe that this situation is sufficiently general to warrant general intervention in the decision to merge, or any other business decision; and in any event acceptance of an official right to intervene in private decisions on the basis of information which cannot be released to, or assessed by, others can hardly be regarded as a healthy basis on which to regulate the operation of business.

Conflict of interests within business firms

A further rationale has considerably more cogency: it derives from the position of the managers or senior executives in the modern business firm. It has been recognised for centuries that an owner who employed a manager to look after his property ran the risk that the manager would discover ways to increase his wellbeing at his expense. But the employer had the right and the power to demand a full accounting from the employee, and to dismiss him if not satisfied with the result.

[16]

In many large modern corporations, however, the ownership interest is not the property of one man, or even two or three, but is sub-divided among thousands of people and institutions, each one owning only a tiny fraction of the outstanding shares. One such owner may suspect that things are not going as well as they might with the firm but, by himself, he has no effective power to compel the managers to justify their actions. In order to stand a chance of doing so, he would have to act in unison with his fellow owners; but the costs of contacting and persuading them that action is called for are likely to be very high relative to the gain that a small owner could expect through the increase in the value of his shares. Even if all owners believe their firm could be operated more profitably, it is quite possible that no *one* of them will think it worth his while to initiate corrective action.

But even if one should do so, the odds are stacked against success. Any other small owner will calculate that, since his share is so small relative to the total, it will make very little difference to the success of the venture whether or not he shares its costs; and that he will in any event receive the fruits of success through the increase in the value of his investment in the firm. There is thus a conflict between the interests of each individual shareholder and the interests of the group of owners as a whole, and it will be difficult—perhaps impossible—to co-ordinate group action.

So the argument runs, and it appears to provide a rebuttal for the classical proposition that the self-interest of owners is sufficient to ensure the efficient operation of business firms. The actions which *owners* would take in their business may indeed be those which would best serve the community at large; but it is *managers*, who have no apparent incentive to maximise returns to the owners, who make the decisions.

Several conclusions are possible. One view—more radical on paper, though not necessarily in practice, than the trend of policy—is that, insofar as the corporate system seems to work well on the whole, it does so without the assistance of the owners, who are unnecessary for its effective functioning (and may even hinder it) and can be disposed of without ill-consequence.[1] The most recent exponent of this position is Mr R. L. Marris:

[1] For example, A. A. Berle and G. C. Means, *The Modern Corporation and Private Property*, Macmillan, New York, 1932, p. 87; R. A. Gordon, *Business Leadership in the Large Corporation*, The Brookings Institution, Washington, D.C., 1945, p. 350.

'If we were to "restructure" our economic system so that the units of production were endowed with the social norm of growth maximisation (subject to financial constraints), and were freed from the embarrassments of stockholders and other trappings of private property, manipulation of the rules to offset various kinds of built-in bias, and generally foster a good society, would be much easier. We would be freed from the inhibitions and costs resulting from our archaic but powerful system of assigning a private owner or part owner to most of our means of production'.[1]

But the more pragmatic view implicit in British policy is equally logical if the premise is accepted: that, since it is not known how managers will behave, it is reasonable to check their competence and past performance before allowing them to proceed with more ambitious investment projects; and to ensure that managers judged to be good by the IRC should command more resources than they otherwise would.

Managers and take-over bids

The validity of these propositions crucially depends upon the accuracy of the assertion that corporate executives have substantial latitude in their use of corporate funds. One may agree that managers will not be substantially impeded by the possibility of direct action by small stockholders; but this does not exhaust the possible bounds on their latitude. Several possible constraints have been proposed,[2] but there is only one constraint which can, in principle, compel managers to attempt to maximise returns to the owners. It is the take-over bid—tolerably familiar after the excitements of the last few years, though its place in the system is not so well recognised.

Suppose the managers of a corporation operated it so incompetently or transferred so much of the profits away from dividends for the owners that its shares were half the price they could have been if returns to the owners were maximised. Could

[1] R. L. Marris, 'Galbraith, Solow and the Truth about Corporations', *The Public Interest*, Spring 1968, p. 46.
[2] My 'Capitalism and the Corporation', *Economica*, November 1969, contains a discussion of other possible controls: in particular those stemming from the existence of a board of directors and from the possibility that the firm may wish to raise outside capital.

such a firm really exist? On *a priori* grounds, at least, it seems doubtful. If each share has a vote in the election of the board of directors, so that a person who owns (say) 50 per cent of the outstanding shares can elect a majority of the board and so exercise control of the managers, any individual or institution that purchases a controlling interest could roughly double the value of his investment by forcing the managers to maximise returns to the owners—or by replacing them with his own appointees who would act in accordance with his wishes. In other words, managers cannot afford to assume that because the ownership interest in their firms is fragmented, it will *continue* to be fragmented however they behave. They may find themselves facing tougher opposition than scattered stockholders with individually insignificant holdings.

The possibility of take-over will not only place a direct constraint on managers. It will also add force to the other limitations on their action. First, it sharpens the risk to directors that they will be exposed as having been associated with a firm in which the integrity of the management is suspect. When outside interests are concerned with the possibility of buying control, managers cannot afford to have men of known integrity leave the board, and to replace them with figure-heads would be to arouse suspicion that all was not well.

Second, the capital market constraint is tightened. Managers' freedom to use retained earnings for the finance of investments is limited because retentions at too high a level will reduce the market value of shares and thus increase the risk of take-over. Nor can managers afford to ignore potentially profitable investments which require outside capital. Insofar as a part of the potential value of a firm consists in the investment opportunities expected to be open to it, to ignore them would be to risk a fall in share prices below the potential value of the firm. Again, the risk of take-over would be increased.

Take-over bids and mergers

Even if the take-over mechanism is fully effective, however, its operation may not be obvious to a casual observer. There are few private individuals who can contemplate the purchase of a corporation, and most of the potential purchasers of corporations will in practice be other corporations, the managers of which have at their disposal the capital-raising ability of their firm and a pool of entrepreneurial ability. For them, lucrative investments provide an excellent means of increasing their remuneration.

This does not impede the effectiveness of the take-over threat, but it complicates the identification of cases in which an incompetent or profligate management is getting its reward. If private persons were doing the bidding, for example, no one would think that the purpose of the bid was to achieve economies of scale or to increase monopoly power: a mere change of ownership could not produce either effect. But when one corporation bids for another, there is almost always someone who is prepared to argue one position or the other, and the argument achieves additional plausibility because, when it is at all feasible, the managers of the joining firms will claim that the reason for their decision lies in the potential economies of scale, even when it is due to the misuse by one of them of their corporation's assets.

The reason for this subterfuge is that contested bids are likely to be expensive for both bidder and defender. Both have incentives to reach agreement if that is at all possible. Further, it is no part of the purpose of the managers of the bidding firm to punish or humiliate their erring counterparts. When agreement can be reached, therefore, the merger—for so it will appear—will be announced in such a way that the maximum of face is saved for the managers of the firm being taken over. Thus, there are likely to be assertions of economies of scale or other vaguely specified benefits to owners and to the economy.

The aim of the bidding firm is to buy the other firm at the lowest possible price. The relevant question is whether it is cheaper to obtain the acquiescence of the incumbent managers to their bid or to go ahead without it. The cost of obtaining agreement will probably take the form of contracts assuring the incumbents of their conditions of employment with the joined firm: salaries, pensions, stock option plans, and terms governing the termination of contract, and all this may be expensive. But to go ahead against the opposition of the sitting management will probably make it necessary to offer a higher price for the shares of their firm—depending on the extent to which the incumbents can persuade the owners that the bid is not in their interest—and gives rise to the risk that the bid will not be successful at any price the bidders are prepared to offer.

Some evidence on these propositions is offered in a recent study by Professor H. B. Rose and G. D. Newbould.[1] They found that:

'For the 24 uncontested acquisitions in our subsample the average premium over pre-bid price was 20 per cent; for those contested by directors only it was 60 per cent, and for those bringing a third party to the scene the average premium over pre-acquisition price was 55 per cent'.

The managers of the firm threatened with take-over also have incentives to compromise. If they agree to the bid, they will be doing so from a position of weakness and, although they can probably make some accommodation which leaves them with financial security, they will lose their independence of action and probably finish up as premature pensioners with no real influence or find themselves working under stringent supervision. The bidding firm will not be prepared to pay them more than the excess of the cost of their opposition to the bid over the market value of the services they can provide after the bid has succeeded. The managers are therefore likely to be in a worse position if they do not fight than if they can maintain their independence untrammelled. On the other hand, if they fight and lose, they will have nothing but the contracts they have made with the firm—though these might be quite substantial—and a tarnished reputation. In many cases, discretion will seem the better part of valour.

An agreed bid, therefore, may result from the majority of cases in which a take-over was threatened. When it does, the result will be an ostensibly amicable merger, complete with photographs of the chief executives of the two firms shaking hands. This is not to suggest, of course, that amicable mergers do not occur. The point is, rather, that the chairmen of two merging firms will always smile at each other; but sometimes one smile may be false.

It would not be correct, therefore, to attempt to infer the importance of the take-over limitation on managerial freedom from the number of contested bids. These are merely a dramatic illustration of its existence: to think that there is no more to the matter would be to mistake the tip for the iceberg.

[1] H. B. Rose and G. D. Newbould, 'The 1967 Take-Over Boom', *Moorgate and Wall Street*, Autumn 1967, p. 23.

III. THE MARKET IN CORPORATE CONTROL[1]

It is not particularly illuminating to pose theoretical possibilities against one another. Is the market in corporate control effective or not?

The question boils down to a simple matter of fact: are the managers of firms from which the owners could derive more income able to maintain their freedom of action over long periods? As is often true of simple questions, it is much easier to state the question than to find a satisfactory answer.

Identifying causes of unprofitability

It is simple enough to identify firms which are relatively unprofitable—which display a low rate of return on capital or for which the price of a share is low relative to some valuation of assets. It is much more difficult to determine whether the causes are beyond the control of the managers of the firm, or whether the situation could be improved by replacing the current managers; that is, whether there are alternative managers available at a price which would make it worthwhile to hire them in the place of the incumbents. The best that can be done is to adopt some more or less arbitrary convention: for example, that all firms in an 'industry' have the same opportunities and *could* earn the same rate of profit.

Nor is it easy to discover whether the managers of such firms have, in practice, been able to maintain their independence. Hitherto, most of the discussion has been in terms of an outright purchase of one firm by another; and this situation is easy enough to identify. But the accumulation of a small fraction of the outstanding shares—say, 5 or 10 per cent—by a person, a firm, or an institution which has the ability either to mount or to initiate a full-scale raid may be sufficient to cause a substantial change in managerial policies, but may also be quite difficult to discover. Indeed, if the market in corporate control were efficient, one might expect most of the transactions in it to be of this nature:

[1] This term was coined by Professor H. G. Manne, 'Mergers and the Market for Corporate Control', *Journal of Political Economy*, April 1965.

it is unlikely that firms which could profitably be purchased would then be allowed to hang about until someone was sufficiently confident to make an offer for all, or a large part of, the outstanding shares.

These qualifications reduce the force of the scanty evidence that exists, but there is some indication that the market in corporate control is not entirely effective. A recent study,[1] using US data, suggests that the ratio of stock market price of a share to net tangible assets per share of firms known to have been subject to attempts to buy control was about two-thirds of that for unraided firms in comparable industries: and that many firms with a low ratio survive without identifiable intervention. Both of these findings would suggest that managers have considerable latitude.

On the other hand, insofar as the comparison is between managerial firms, these results also suggest that many managements do not use the freedom which the market allows to divert returns from the owners. One possible (and plausible) explanation is *internal* constraints—say, the board of directors—and that as a result they seek to create a situation in which their remuneration through salaries, pensions, stock options and so on will be as large as possible. In most cases, this would probably produce the sort of business decisions the owners themselves would take; or at least as good an approximation as is necessary to hide any differences in behaviour among errors in the data.

A more indirect approach is to see whether there are significant differences of performance between owner-controlled and manager-controlled firms. Substantial differences would imply that the market in corporate control is not efficient; no differences might mean it is efficient. But it does not, because of the internal constraints, *necessarily* imply this. Studies of this kind are also subject to difficulties of interpretation. For example, the comparison may be between elements of new (or recently successful) and old-established firms, or between the founders of successful firms, who may be men of exceptional ability, and managers who are relatively less capable; and both of these factors would tend to bias the comparison in favour of the owner-controlled firms.

[1] B. Hindley, 'Separation of Ownership and Control in the Modern Corporation', *Journal of Law and Economics*, April 1970.

At least three comparisons of this type have been made, all using US data, for different industries and periods. Only one of them has reported statistically significant differences between the performance of owner-controlled and managerial firms; and it was the managerial firms that appear to have performed less well.[1] The others found differences in the same direction, but these were not statistically significant.

Can the market be improved?

This evidence is clearly not conclusive. It certainly does not warrant the assertion that the corporate system is inefficient, nor the formulation of general policies based on its inefficiency. But it also fails to demonstrate that all is as it should be. We shall therefore proceed to a second question: can the market in corporate control be improved?[2]

If it can, there are two obvious places to look for the improvement. The first is in the amount of *information* available to the market, and the second in the amount of *capital* necessary to displace an incumbent management. The object is not to displace managements, unless incompetent, but rather to increase the risk which competent managements run if they act against the interest of the owners.

Information is necessary for two purposes: to enable ordinary owners and purchasers of shares to make the most accurate possible assessment of their value, and potential purchasers of control to make an accurate assessment of the income stream if

[1] R. Joseph Monsen, John S. Chiu and David E. Cooley, 'The Effect of the Separation of Ownership and Control on the Performance of the Large Firm', *Quarterly Journal of Economics*, August 1968. The others are Hindley, *ibid.*, and David R. Kamarschen, 'The Influence of Ownership and Control on Profit Rates', *American Economic Review*, June 1968.

[2] When firms have market power, and there are externalities, the allocation of resources *may* be better when managers consult their own interests rather than those of the owners. They may, for example, wish to obtain revenue rather than profits and thus not fully exploit the firm's monopoly power. Or they may wish to grow fast, investing more in research and development than would be most profitable from the point of view of the owners. The marginal social gains from research expenditure may be larger than the marginal private gains so that profit-maximising firms would undertake less than would be socially ideal: and the community could gain even if the owners were less well off. But if managers can act contrary to the interests of owners and yet do good by society at large, a failure of *government* policy is implied. The more general needs served by the actions of managers would be better answered by a more stringent anti-monopoly policy, or more effective support for 'R and D'. For public policy there is no ambiguity: it *is* desirable that managers should act as though the interests of owners were paramount.

the firm were under their control. To some extent the information required for these purposes overlaps, but usually it would be deeper and more detailed for the second. It is here that the main problem lies.

The first requirement is that there should be much more detailed disclosure of accounting information. Rather than presenting consolidated accounts, firms should be required to break down their results to the smallest feasible unit, certainly to the level of divisions, and preferably to the level of the constituent parts of divisions. Information of this kind should be automatically accessible both to ordinary share owners and to potential purchasers of control.[1]

But although this information would probably help potential purchasers of control, it would not necessarily be sufficient. They want to know not only what is happening, but also what *could* happen were they in control. It is much more difficult to provide information of this kind, but one possibility would be for the law to require corporations to adopt a voting structure so that the owner of a relatively small fraction of the outstanding shares— 5 or 10 per cent—could be sure of electing at least one director to the board with full access to information. A potential purchaser of control would then have access to accurate inside information at a rather lower cost than is now possible; the capital cost of exerting pressure on an erring management would be reduced.

Operations in the market in corporate control inevitably require large amounts of capital. A person who wishes to obtain control of a firm must either buy shares and votes, or undertake the expensive task of persuading the owners to give him their votes without purchasing the shares. The latter course, the proxy fight, is likely to be particularly important in large corporations. Were General Motors to become avoidably inefficient, for example, a proxy fight would probably be essential to unseat the incumbent management; it would be exceedingly difficult, if not impossible, to construct a financial coalition to purchase control outright.

---

[1] The Monopolies Commission suggests (in its appendix to the reports on the Allied-Unilever and Rank-De La Rue mergers at paras. 32 and 33) that more information should be available. It concludes its discussion with the comment: 'We realise that the availability of this additional information could make it easier for acquisitive firms to identify firms capable of being taken over but, insofar as this is undesirable, it is a risk which in our opinion should be accepted'.

Professor Harold Rose, *Disclosure in Company Accounts*, Eaton Paper 1, Institute of Economic Affairs, second edition, 1965, gives an excellent discussion of the problems involved in disclosure.

Improvements in the proxy fight mechanism provide one means of reducing the capital requirements of imposing a constraint on managers. The rules of the game should not be formulated in such a way as to increase the costs to their challengers. For example, an up-to-date list of shareholders should be automatically available to any one of them. But a more important question concerns the right of incumbent managers to draw on corporate funds in their defence against a proxy fight. If they did not have this right, their bargaining position *vis-à-vis* potential take-over bidders would be substantially weakened, and the leverage which could be exerted by the owner of, say, a 10 per cent share would correspondingly be increased.

While this procedure would reduce the scope of managers to act against the owners' interest, managers might object to it on the ground that they would also become exposed to 'irresponsible' attacks against the interests of the owners. But it is difficult to see that a management which has been successfully acting in the interests of the owners would be vulnerable to such an attack; it is managers who have not been acting in this way who would be exposed, and there is then no reason to suppose the identity of interest between owners and managers which the managers' right to protect themselves with corporate funds presumes. Why should the owners finance the efforts of the incumbents to stay in power, and why should they not pass judgement upon the responsibility of the challengers?

Splitting the conglomerates

Large corporations will always pose a problem, and, particularly in dealing with large conglomerates, a further change might be desirable. Few firms or organisations are able to take over a very large firm in its entirety, even though it might be highly profitable to do so. There may be many more prepared to bid for parts of it, and since many large firms encompass separable activities, this course should be technically feasible. It should be made possible, therefore, for one firm to propose directly to the owners of another that it should purchase a division or a subsidiary or any other separable part. Fuller disclosure of accounting results would enable the owners to compare the past income stream deriving from a constituent operation with the purchase price offered by the bidder. There is no reason to suppose that they would not be able to arrive at a rational conclusion; but, under this threat, managers would probably be willing to discuss the sale of their less profitable operations without recourse to the owners. If this course were successful, it would eliminate any need to worry about large conglomerates—and many other large firms—lagging in their performance yet safe from correction because of the difficulties of raising capital to buy control.

The emergence of the corporate system does require adjustments in the institutions affecting business firms. The direct guarantee of the interest of decision-takers in the efficiency of owner-controlled firms is replaced, in the corporate system, with a subtler set of incentives, which require different institutional reinforcements. The proposals above are an attempt to suggest the type of institutional arrangements required, and the direction in which thought should go. Even if the power of managers is a pressing problem, there is no reason why it should continue to be one.

Yet to curb managerial discretion by this means would be to encourage corporate mergers. Is there any conflict between the 'public interest' in other aspects of merger and the stronger use of the take-over threat against lax or incompetent managers?

IV. POLICY ON CONGLOMERATE MERGER

Economic thinking about merger has traditionally been based on the idea that mergers may be good if they yield economies of scale, or bad if they increase the monopoly power of the combining firms. For the present purpose it is convenient to start with 'conglomerate mergers', which have recently been the subject of extensive discussion in Britain and the United States.[1] A conglomerate merger occurs when two firms engaged in technically unrelated activities unite. For example, a meat packer buys a manufacturer of locomotives, or a soft drink manufacturer an airline. Most of the 'problem' for public policy occurs because such mergers are difficult to explain in terms of monopoly or economies of scale; and it is hard to make sensible policy to regulate phenomena whose causes are imperfectly understood.

[1] Donald Turner, 'Conglomerate Mergers and Section 7 of the Clayton Act', *Harvard Law Review*, May 1965, gives a good account of the problem in the US context.

With a little analytical ingenuity, one can find ways in which there may be either reductions in costs or enhanced monopoly power. Thus meat packers are important customers of railroads, who are buyers of locomotives. The meat packer may be able to use his buying power with the railroads to compel them to purchase locomotives made by his new acquisition, and thus steal an unfair march on competitor locomotive manufacturers. And even soft drink firms and airlines share the need for office staff and advertising and so on, so that the joined firms may be able to reduce the amount they spend on them. Also, of course, a large firm may be able to acquire capital more cheaply than a smaller one. In an inter-dependent economy, an imaginative and diligent analyst can always find connections between any two firms, and is therefore able to unearth possibilities of economies of scale or enhanced monopoly power.

But very few economic analysts—if any—would assert that connections of this kind *explain* the bulk of conglomerate mergers. They may be *consequences* of such mergers, but as *explanations* they are less than convincing. Indeed, it is unlikely that the connections would even have been sought had conglomerate merger been, in the past, the typical phenomenon rather than horizontal and vertical merger—that is, mergers between firms engaged in obviously related activities. In these cases it is plausible to suppose that the connections provide both the cause and the consequence of the merger. But to restrict the analysis of conglomerate merger to these factors is to put new wine into old bottles.

Possible causes of conglomerate merger

Take a hypothetical example. Suppose that a cheese producer wholly owned by one person merges with a chalk manufacturer whose shareholders accept cash for their shares, so that the new firm is still wholly owned by one person. There are then no problems arising from the position of managers (discussed in pp. 34–37).

There is an obvious presumption that the owner of the cheese firm *expects* to gain from the merger, but he might hold this opinion for a variety of reasons. Some of the more important are:

(1) He believes that whatever monopoly power the chalk manufacturer possesses could be exploited more profitably.

(2) The costs of output of the chalk firm could be reduced by more effective management.

(3) The profitability of the chalk firm could be increased by a change in its marketing policies: for example, it might be spending either too much or too little on advertising.

(4) The acquiring firm might own factors of production which could be exploited more profitably if they were combined with factors owned by the acquired firm. For example, the established brand name of one firm might profitably be associated with the good but unknown product of the other. Or the cheese maker might want to expand his operations into a foreign market in which the chalk manufacturer has a special marketing expertise. And so on.

Many of these categories tend to blur at the edges, and the first three could be considered as special cases of the fourth. This does not affect the argument, and there are relevant distinctions between the four groups.

The list of conglomerate mergers is likely to be a particularly fruitful source of mergers which are, in essence, concealed take-over bids. This is precisely because they cannot be explained in terms of 'industrial logic';[1] so that a probably more correct explanation is relatively unprofitable operation by the managers of one of the firms. But the four possibilities listed above provide ample ground for a genuinely amicable merger. The first three are consistent with unprofitable operation. But there is no ground for asserting that all conglomerate mergers conceal the coercion of one management by the other. If it were necessary to sort out entirely voluntary mergers from those forced by one side in the transaction, there would be considerable difficulty. We must therefore inquire whether there is any reason to prevent particular mergers, and whether it might, in that case, be necessary to discover whether the merger was voluntary or not.

---

[1] The term is used (though not originated) by the Monopolies Commission in its appendix to the Allied-Unilever and Rank-De La Rue reports (para. 21). It is a somewhat loaded phrase insofar as no one (presumably) would wish to support a merger which displayed industrial illogic. It is discussed in more detail below (p. 33).

The hypothetical merger might raise objections on the ground that since the expected profitability of the purchase might stem from the tougher exploitation of the chalk firm's monopoly power, there is no presumption of social gain. The point is valid—though its force is diminished by the reflection that one might reasonably expect a management not sharp enough to exploit its selling advantages to be too dull to minimise the costs of its output. But, accepting the objection, one could not restrict its application to mergers between two firms. Exactly the same argument would hold true if the purchaser of the chalk maker owned no business. If, say, an accountant was the potential purchaser, would it be sensible to prevent the purchase on the ground that he looked as though he would operate it more profitably than the previous owner? It is difficult to conceive of a rational policy cast in these terms. If this is so, why should such a policy become rational if the potential purchaser is not an accountant but the owner of another, unrelated business?

Yet what other arguments could there be for official inter-vention in the hypothetical merger? Mistakes by the acquirer have been mentioned (pp. 10–12).[1] The two remaining possibilities seem to be that the new owner might take actions which affect the government's regional policy, or that it might take actions adverse to the balance of payments.[2]

Suppose it is definitely known that the cheese maker, as part of his programme of reducing the chalk maker's costs of production, would close down some plants, possibly in parts of the country where official policy was designed to increase employment oppor-tunities. It seems clear that this would be a foolish criterion on which to reject the merger. It is necessary to distinguish between the case to be made for assisting people who are harmed by the introduction of more efficient methods of production—wherever

[1] In a sense, however, policy has already been based on errors of judgement. The Monopolies Commission recommended against the proposed Rank-De La Rue merger on the ground that '. . . We think that it [Rank] has underestimated the difficulties with which it would be faced and the risks it would run' (para. 105). The Commission is somewhat evasive about whether it is asserting that its judge-ment is superior to that of Rank, or merely that it has better information (para. 88). But none of the information that it indicates it has would have been prejudicial to De La Rue were it given to Rank, so that one must favour the former interpretation.
[2] Seven of the 116 questions in *Mergers (op. cit.)* deal with employment and 21 with the balance of payments.

they may be—and the means of financing the assistance to be given. There is no doubt that a strong case can be made for assistance; but it would be absurd to insist that the firm which had introduced an increase in efficiency should foot the bill on that account, thus discouraging its introduction in the first place. To prevent one firm from acquiring another which is operating high-cost plants because the acquirer would concentrate production in lower-cost plants, or to insist as a condition of allowing the merger that it should not do so, is simply to insist that the owners of the inefficient firm should continue to pay a tax (in the form of lower returns) in support of the government's employment policy.

It would certainly be hard to defend this policy on grounds of equity; and it cannot be very effective. Why should the laying-off of workers be an occasion for intervening in the decision to merge? Men are just as unemployed whether they are laid off by old managers or new. Concern about that should manifest itself in a general policy on plant closures and lay-offs, not as a criterion for allowing a particular merger to proceed.

The balance of payments provides, in Britain, a case for or against almost anything, and this distorts discussion of public policy to an absurd extent. This is true of merger policy. Here, as elsewhere, it is both wasteful and foolish to try to replace a sensible balance-of-payments policy by short-term, *ad hoc* responses to problems which require thought about longer-term consequences.

The basic policy mistake is the same in both cases. Government has particular objectives: a different distribution of employment opportunities or a surplus in the balance of payments. To achieve these goals, its most efficient course is to alter the signals transmitted to decision-makers through the price system: devalue or revalue, say, and either subsidise or tax employment in the appropriate areas. That government feels it necessary to intervene in an *ad hoc* way should be interpreted as an admission of its failure to effect the appropriate changes. But worse, to intervene in one particular kind of decision on these grounds is an extremely inefficient and wasteful substitute for the required policy. The objective should be to obtain the desired ends at the lowest possible cost to the community at large; and to intervene in mergers on these grounds is likely to be a socially expensive means of achieving them—if indeed they can be either achieved or

[31]

furthered *via* that route. Merger policy should be concerned with what merger primarily affects: the efficiency with which industrial resources are used. Attention should not be distracted from this criterion by the undoubted importance of other policy goals, in the attainment of which other policies are most appropriate.

It would be difficult to construct, on these grounds, a persuasive case that the country's economic welfare would be improved by any form of government intervention in the decision of the two firms to merge. Since there is a possibility of loss—through increased exploitation of the acquired firm's monopoly power or through miscalculation by the acquiring firm—a government with infinite resources and a large number of wise and omniscient unemployed men might find it worthwhile to strive for perfection; but we are a long way from that situation, and it is difficult to believe that government could not find a better use for the resources and wise men it can command.

Problems arising from more extensive diversification

This situation would not in principle be changed if the cheese producer purchased, in addition to the chalk firm, a steel mill, cotton mill, a shipping line, a television set manufacturer, and a chain of department stores. But it may be changed in practice. If several firms were behaving in the same way as the (erstwhile) cheese maker, policy-makers would probably be inclined to take more account of the situation than if a few small firms were merging with one other in technically unrelated fields; and the interpretations of what was going on might be changed.

In the context of the analysis presented earlier in this *Paper*,[1] the appearance of firms which spent much of their resources on purchasing other firms would be explicable as specialisation in the function of taking over firms operated at less than full profitability, and therefore undervalued by the stock market relatively to their potential value. As with any other profitable activity, one would expect the development of specialists. Other interpretations are possible, however, and a popular one would run in terms of the overweening ambition of business men combined with the obtuseness of shareholders. I shall return to it (pp. 34–37).

[1] Above, pp. 19–21.

From the point of view of policy-makers, the creation of such firms might give rise to two complaints. The first, which might come from business men as well as politicians and civil servants, is that there is no industrial logic in the mergers. On our explanation of the mergers, of course, this is quite true but also quite irrelevant. (And one might note in passing that, on our explanation, business men should be expected to protest at the unchecked rise of such firms—their complaints would be an indication of the success of the market in tightening the constraints on managers.)

The logic of 'industrial logic'

But the idea of 'industrial logic' is worth pursuing a little further. It is connected with the view that a business man's function is to produce steel, or shoes, or cans of meat, or whatever line he happens to be in. This may be a comforting view for many business men, but it is a fallacy: a business man's function is to produce profits. The reason for this is very simple: profits are the only indication that a business man is producing what people want.[1] A shirtmaker, for example, who produces garments which will wear for ever, but which are styled in a way that would appeal to late Victorians, is simply wasting resources. Few people want such shirts, as he will discover by the failure of his efforts to show a profit. It would be better for both the community and himself that he should decide to produce shirts that people do want—and start showing a profit.

If the switch to producing shirts that people want can be achieved by merger—by control of the firm's marketing policy moving into other hands—why should one look for 'industrial logic'? If industrial logic means (as presumably it must) that the integration of the technical operations of two firms will lead to a reduction in their total costs, it is a splendid characteristic of mergers which possess it. But to make it the sole criterion by which a merger is judged would be foolish.

---

[1] It has already been noted that that a business is making a profit does not demonstrate that its actions are laudable from a social point of view. The earnings may derive from its monopoly power, for example. But the appropriate response to this is not to decry business men who have sufficient energy and initiative to make profits, but to provide an institutional framework in which actions that produce profits are also in the social interest.

The second possible complaint is based on the putative absence of limits to the growth of a firm prepared to move into completely diverse fields of enterprise. If firms are limited to one industry, even if the term 'industry' is defined broadly, there is a 'natural' limit to their size. If firms can spread across industry lines, this limit disappears. If we permit conglomerate merger, therefore, might we not finish up in a situation in which a small number of firms—50? 10? one?—control the entire economy?

Even if one accepted this as a plausible outcome, its significance from an *economic* point of view is open to question. For example, if the economy contained only 50 firms, but each held 2 per cent of every market, the approximation of perfect competition might be better than is now the case with many more firms than 50. Economic theory has always dealt with the problem of size relative to *markets*, not to the economy as a whole; so long as there is effective means of controlling size relative to markets, there is little it has to say about size *per se*.

From a social and political point of view, however, an economy dominated by a handful of firms is not the same as an economy with thousands of firms; and other things equal, some people would prefer one and some the other. I would myself prefer many firms, and there would probably be little economic loss from reducing the size of many of the larger firms in the economy. But this is a matter for a general decision on size, not for preventing conglomerate mergers *per se*.[1]

Problems arising from the power of managers

Neither of the possible objections based on the number of diverse acquisitions made by a firm should affect the view that there is no case for intervention in decisions regarding particular conglomerate mergers. But much of the argument presumes that firms will be operated in the interests of their owners. It was appropriate to base the analysis of the hypothetical mergers on this assumption, since it was supposed that the cheese firm had a single owner, and it was probably a tolerable approximation to say that his main concern was to

---

[1] It is one of the ironies of Labour Party ideology that its members, having largely abandoned the idea of widespread nationalisation, but still believing in the widespread economies of scale on which it was based, support public subsidies for the creation of big private businesses *via* the IRC.

maximise his wealth. In practice, however, most of the larger firms which merge their interests in the modern world do not have a single owner but are under managerial control. Firms bidding for the control of other firms are therefore open to exactly the same criticism as other corporations: there is no reason to suppose that the interests of the owners are necessarily paramount when their executives take decisions.

Thus suppose that the cheese firm had thousands of owners, none holding a large enough interest to influence the managers. Suppose the managers preferred to run a larger and more diversified firm and embarked on a programme of acquisitions. Could one still say there was no case for prior government approval?

The answer depends upon the efficiency of the take-over market. If it is very efficient, so that small deviations from full potential profits induce outside intervention in the affairs of the firm, the case for official intervention is very weak. If the managers of the cheese firm were making poor purchases, so that their acquisitions returned less than the market rate of return on the investment,[1] the firm's shares would fall in price, causing a discrepancy between potential value and market price, accumulation of shares by potential purchasers of control would start, and the managers would either have to curtail their acquisitions—and possibly dispose of some of those already made—or face a full-scale bid. If the market is inefficient, this process will not occur or will be so slow and uncertain that the managers have a good deal of latitude.

There might then be an argument for official intervention, because the possibility that managers will take socially undesirable decisions is increased. But the important point is that intervention should neither take the form of, nor have the effect of preventing, conglomerate mergers or increasing their costs. Even managers consulting their own interests have incentives to make the most profitable purchases possible; they will therefore seek to acquire firms which they believe to be undervalued by the stock market relatively to their potential value, so providing an incentive for other managers to avoid that situation. It may be that a more desirable purchaser could be found for their acquisition (though he

[1] If it was necessary to finance the acquisitions by the issue of new shares, the capital market would also provide a constraint: a firm cannot continue indefinitely to issue shares for investments which do not earn a market rate of return.

did not think them worth the price) or that the acquired firm would better remain independent (though its owners did not think it worth the price). But whatever the criticism it is likely to be implicitly based on the *imperfection* of the take-over market; and that clearly cannot provide a sensible reason for impeding the market still further. On the contrary, to avoid adverse effects of conglomerate merger the appropriate policy is to attempt to improve that market.

In its report on the proposed Rank-De La Rue merger, however, the Monopolies Commission comes dangerously close to the opinion that the market should be entirely suspended (paragraph 82):

'There is one general point which we wish to make here. Appraisal of the public interest in the effect of mergers can include their effect both on competition and on efficiency. The argument was put to us in the present case that if we could find no adverse effects on competition, the market, that is to say the stock market, and not the Commission, was the best judge of efficiency. If the shareholders of the firm being bid for accepted the offer, then by implication, they took the view that the bidding firm would use the assets of the other more efficiently and their judgement on this point should be regarded by the Commission as conclusive. We reject this argument. In the first place, and this is specially true of a contested merger, the Commission may, and probably will, have more information than the market on which to base an assessment of the likely outcome. In the second place . . . shareholders faced with an offer are more likely to be concerned with its financial implications for themselves (including tax considerations) than with the efficiency with which resources are to be used'.

This statement entirely misses the point. Of course stockholders will only be concerned with the financial implications for themselves; but the question the Commission neglects to ask is why the firm is prepared to make the bid. It is against the managers of that firm that the Commission must compare its judgement, and it is reasonable to think that *their* judgement is superior to that of the Commission. It is not clear what 'information' the Commission would have which could not be released either to shareholders (so that they realised that the price offered for their shares was too low relative to their company's prospects) or to the bidding firm (so that it realised that its estimate of the potential value of the firm it sought to purchase was too high). Certainly the information on which the Commission largely based its rejection of the Rank-De La Rue merger—that De La Rue executives might quit if Rank took over—could have been given to Rank without prejudice to De La Rue's interests; but it seems unlikely that Rank's decision would have been changed since it must have expected De La Rue resignations in any event, and would quite likely have encouraged them.

The Commission *could* have argued that there may be sufficient latitude for managers to indulge their own whims and that it is therefore reasonable for the Commission to check that their decisions coincide with 'the public interest'. But this leads to the question of how their putative freedom to act against the interests of the owners—and society—can be reduced. It is not at all obvious that random merger references to the Monopolies Commission are the best way to attain that goal.

V. POLICY ON VERTICAL AND HORIZONTAL MERGER

The new element added to the merger problem when we turn from conglomerate to horizontal and vertical merger is that the technical connections between the activities in which the firms are engaged are clear. Two highly plausible explanations of merger are thereby added to those discussed in Section III: firms may wish to merge in order to increase their monopoly power, or to attain the benefits of economies of scale or integration. These explanations do not exclude each other—a merger may contain elements of both.[1]

It is here that the real problems raised by merger occur. Mergers contracted in order to attain economies of scale or integration are clearly not undesirable on that ground. The sole ground for

---

[1] It should be said that the bulk of mergers probably have little to do with any of these factors, but are due to the desire of their owner-manager to convert his ownership interest to some other form of asset. The explanations in the text are pertinent when one is discussing mergers between firms which have a widely dispersed ownership.

presumption of social loss from merger is that, by merging, firms in an industry may increase their power to set prices without any offsetting reduction in their costs of production.

Self-imposed monopolies

Much of Britain's problem with monopoly and merger is probably self-imposed. There are few industries in which economies of scale are so important that efficient production requires a high level of concentration in world markets. There are many more in which economies of scale require a high level of concentration in British markets. When Britain erects high tariff barriers, or impedes the importation of foreign goods by any other artifice, she creates a situation in which monopoly is likely to become a much more important element in the economy than is inherently necessary.

But insofar as the political constraints on action to reduce artificial import restrictions (which at the moment mainly stem from balance-of-payment considerations) are effective, it is to the good that a stringent policy for controlling merger is pursued. At the moment the main agency for dealing with suspect cases is the Monopolies Commission.

The Monopolies and Mergers Act, 1965 gave the Board of Trade the power to refer a suspect merger to the Commission for detailed inquiry. Before that, only references of an industry with a 'dominant firm' could be made, a dominant firm being one which possessed more than one-third of the market in the UK.

A. HORIZONTAL MERGER

Mergers which do nothing other than increase the level of concentration in an industry are, *per se*, undesirable. If all possible economies of scale were exhausted within the current structure of industries, the simplest way to deal with the problem, and the most effective, would be to ban the purchase of one firm by another in the industry. However, some such purchases would not have any significant effect on the power of firms within the industry to collude or otherwise set price above marginal cost. The appropriate rule would then be that firms could not expand their shares of total sales in the industry made in Britain beyond a specified percentage by merger or acquisition. Firms with a larger market share would not be allowed to expand further by merger.[1]

If there are economies of scale, however, this prohibition would not be entirely satisfactory. The rule might then prevent the attainment of the most efficient scale of production: a cost which might outweigh the gains from closing this path to monopoly.

This loss might not be serious. If there are substantial unexhausted economies of scale they will in time be achieved through the internal expansion of some firms and the withdrawal of others. The loss from applying the rule, therefore, is not likely to continue permanently: it would be the value of the product foregone through less than optimal production between the time at which the economies of scale could have been realised by merger and the time at which they are realised by internal expansion.[2]

Appeals against merger bans?

Nevertheless, it might be desirable to take account of the possibility that such losses could occur by establishing a means of appeal for firms covered by the ban. In order to be exempted, firms wishing to merge would have to demonstrate the possibility of further economies of scale by merging or that the firm to be acquired was on the point of ceasing production, and that no other potential purchaser was available.[3] The latter proviso would simply mean that when an increase in concentration was inevitable through the demise of a firm in an industry, another firm in the industry could make use of its assets.

[1] I would not wish to suggest that the concept of an 'industry' for this purpose (or any other) is completely straightforward. There is room for a good deal of technical discussion on the appropriate definition. However the present monopoly criterion for merger (and dominant-firm) references is phrased in terms of the percentage (one-third) of the supply of goods and services in the hands of the merging companies. All of the definitional difficulties involved must therefore arise under the present legislation; and the additional difficulty raised by the suggested rule would be that the products which constituted a 'good' for the purposes of the legislation would have to be defined before rather than after the fact of a proposed merger. This does not seem too large a cost to undergo in order to let everyone know where they stand.

[2] Oliver E. Williamson, 'Economies as an Antitrust Defense: The Welfare Trade-offs', *American Economic Review*, March 1968, pp. 18–36, provides a technical discussion of these points.

[3] Should it be thought necessary to keep the IRC in existence, it could find a role in sponsoring such appeals. It would in any case be useful to provide the opportunity for critical discussion of the evidence which leads it to believe that it has discovered unexhausted economies of scale.

Given that the loss from disallowing appeals would not be permanent, the appeals agency could afford to apply stringent standards in its examination of the case. It could, for example, ask firms wishing to merge why they had changed their minds about the efficient scale of production since they had constructed their facilities, or what changes in the techniques of production required a larger scale of production. It could expect firms to produce evidence on the structure of foreign industries, or on the relative profitability of large and small firms.

The proposed appeals agency would be in a quite different position from that of the Monopolies Commission under the present system of dealing with merger. The appeals agency would be passing judgement on the validity of a case prepared by firms which knew when they made plans to merge that it would be necessary to appeal before the merger could be consummated. The firms would therefore know what to expect, and what would be expected of them. The agency would have only one criterion: whether a satisfactory case had been presented. The firms themselves would obtain the relevant data, and there is no reason why they should not be asked to expand on points should the agency so wish. A case which failed to satisfy the agency would result in rejection of the appeal: the merger would not then proceed, or, if the threat of increased concentration stemmed from only part of the firms' activities, one of them would have to sell its interests in that area before the merger could proceed.

Under the present system, the Monopolies Commission is asked to balance the effect of a variety of factors; but neither it, nor the firms referred to it, know in advance that the reference will be made, and everyone has to prepare a case from scratch. In order that the reference shall not unduly interfere with the merger process, the time for the inquiry is strictly limited. It is not usually sufficient to collect the kind of data desirable for a sound decision, so that the Commission frequently finds itself faced with bland assurances of impressive economies with no satisfactory means of checking their plausibility. In any event, the Commission is not equipped to handle more than a few cases at a time, and when there are an unusually large number of suspect mergers, it is impossible to refer all of them. Neither the system nor the method provides adequate protection against the danger to the public interest inherent in horizontal merger.

This is not to criticise the Monopolies Commission, which is asked to work in an inappropriate framework. The Commission might itself provide the appeals agency. Alternatively, the agency could be independent of existing institutions.

B. Vertical merger

This proposal would leave firms largely free to engage in vertical mergers, although it would prevent a firm already engaged in vertically-connected markets from expanding its share of them beyond the stated percentage by merger. This is as it should be. There is no clear-cut economic case against vertical mergers. The usual basis of complaint against a vertical merger is that it excludes competitors of the purchaser from either buying from or selling to the acquired company, depending upon whether the integration were backward or forward. For example, the Monopolies Commission, in its Appendix to the Rank-De La Rue report (para. 20), reprinted as Annex 4 to *Mergers* (*op. cit.*), says:

'A vertical merger between companies may bar other potential suppliers from competing for a particular outlet and other outlets from access to a particular source of supply, and this may be against the public interest where it leads to a significant part of a given market being effectively removed from competitive influence'.

The logic of this position would imply that a firm which wished to expand forwards or backwards in the line of production by *internal* means should also be subject to check, for such internal expansion would have exactly the same effect in this respect as vertical integration by merger. However, this argument cannot apply at all if both of the merging firms were monopolists at their respective stages of production, for then neither would have any competition to exclude. In that case—bilateral monopoly—the reason for the merger is likely to be that the two monopolists could not agree on the division of the profits; but the position that would best satisfy either of them would be worse, from the point of view of the community, than that which would best satisfy a single owner of both firms.[1] There is therefore no ground

[1] For a technical discussion of this point see almost any text in intermediate economic theory, e.g., G. J. Stigler, *Theory of Price*, Collier-Macmillan, Third Edition, 1966, p. 207 *et seq.*

for objection to such a merger, although the monopolistic nature of the industry itself may be objectionable, and it may be desirable to seek ways of increasing the number of firms in the market.

(i) Integration backwards

If we suppose that there is a monopoly at one stage and two firms at the other, we can examine the charge that a vertical merger will exclude the other firm from a source of sales or purchases. To be more specific, suppose that a monopolistic retailer is supplied by two manufacturers and that the retailer buys one of the manufacturers, or that a manufacturer buys the retailer. Insofar as the integrated firm seeks to maximise its profits, its policy should be the same in either case.

If economies of scale in manufacturing could be obtained by concentrating all manufacturing within one firm, the retailer would, of course, find it profitable to pursue that policy. He would presumably concentrate his purchases of merchandise with his new acquisition, so excluding the second manufacturer from retail outlets. But this is not against the public interest: less resources would be used in the production of merchandise for the retailer; and the public, confronted with a monopolistic seller whether or not there is a merger of retailer and manufacturer, would probably gain insofar as the retailer, to maximise his joint returns, now has an incentive to reduce his prices as a result of the cheaper supply.

But the existence of two manufacturers would normally imply that the marginal costs of each were rising, and, if so, the retailer would minimise his costs of purchasing any quantity of merchandise by equating the marginal cost of production at his new subsidiary with the price at which the independent manufacturer is prepared to sell. If the two manufacturing firms had been colluding before the merger, holding price to the retailer above their marginal costs, and if the independent manufacturer attempted to maintain the same price after the merger, adherence to this rule would imply that the share of the acquired manufacturer in total sales to the retailer would rise. Once again, however, this would not be against the public interest. The merger might be explained by the retailer's desire to break up the attempt of his suppliers to obtain monopoly profits from him.

Insofar as he succeeds in this objective, he will have an incentive to reduce the price at which he sells the merchandise retail; and presumably this would be in the public interest.

In general, a monopolist at the end of the chain of production could not increase his power to exploit buyers by integrating backwards. He does, however, have an obvious interest in obtaining his supplies as cheaply as possible; and most backward mergers are likely to be a part of his effort to achieve this object— either because there are economies in integration, or attempts at monopoly further down the line of production, or because the firms further back are inefficient.

(ii) Integration forwards

Exactly the same arguments would apply to forward integration. Suppose that we are now dealing with a monopolistic manufacturer who has merged with one of two retailing chains, or with a monopolistic manufacturer of TV tubes, for example, who merged with one of two firms which assemble television sets. The popular argument would be that the newly-integrated firm would deny the independent firm access to a necessary input, thus seizing the whole of the retailing or assembly business for itself.

If the monopolist is in such a powerful position, he can exploit his tube or manufacturing monopoly to the full without forward integration, and his interest lies in obtaining the services complementary with his product (assembling or retailing) at the lowest possible cost. To put the point another way, suppose that the independent firm is prepared to 'sell' him complementary services at a lower price than he can himself provide them. What interest could he have in rejecting this possibility and internalising all operations? The monopolist would have an incentive to eliminate the independent firm only when it is in the public interest that he should do so: that is, when the costs of the service provided by the independent firm can be reduced by concentrating production on one firm. Where this is not possible, the integrated firm has every economic incentive to continue purchases from the outside firm.

Obviously, these conclusions are independent of the number of firms at the non-monopolised stage of production. Nor are they changed if there are several firms at both stages of production. But under the operation of the suggested rule, it would not be possible for either stage to become monopolised by merger without an appearance before the appeals agency. The community would therefore be protected against that possibility.

If an oligopolistic[1] manufacturer buys one of the oligopolistic retail chains which sell his product, it is not clear that he is buying more than the power to cause customers who do not want his brand to go to other retail stores. But suppose he could increase his share of the market through his ownership of retail stores— for example, by instructing the salespeople in the stores to promote his brand. Would this be against the public interest?

If we suppose that the retailer was originally maximising his returns, the analytical problem is why a switch in the purchasing or sales policy should increase the joint returns of the two firms. One possible answer is that the manufacturer has decided to pursue a new marketing policy, which requires the more intensive use of point-of-sale promotion rather than, say, newspaper advertising. This would not provide a satisfactory explanation of the merger, however: why not pay the retailer to provide the services? A more interesting explanation would be that the integrated manufacturer-retailer can now obtain merchandise of his own manufacture more cheaply than could the original retailer. This would happen, for instance, if the manufacturers had been in collusion, so that retailers could not buy their output at marginal cost. Since the integrated firm could obtain its merchandise at marginal cost, it would have an incentive to switch purchases by its retailing subsidiary to its own plant, and to supply more services with them at the retail level. In other words, the merger would signify the introduction of non-price competition where no competition had previously existed; and while it may be still more desirable to have price competition, the merger itself would not be against the public interest even though there might be a strong case for examining the industry structure which produced it.

---

[1] An oligopolistic industry is one in which there are several firms, of which at least one is sufficiently important that it can, by changing its output, affect the price of the industry's product. It is characterised by recognition of interdependence.

None of this is to say that vertical integration cannot raise problems. One possible reason for a desire on the part of a monopolist to integrate forward is so that he can discriminate between purchasers of the final product; and while it is not clear that this manœuvre is against the public interest, it would be an appropriate subject for a 'dominant firm' reference to the Monopolies Commission. Also, vertical integration might provide existing firms with a barrier against new entry. Once again, if this appears to be a problem, it would be an appropriate topic for a 'dominant firm' reference.[1]

Although economies of scale and integration and, in a number of ways, monopoly, are always plausible hypotheses to explain vertical and horizontal merger, it does not follow that all such mergers are attributable to these causes. The list of explanations of conglomerate merger is equally applicable here; and it is quite plausible to suppose that the existence of a firm operated in such a way that it would provide a profitable investment will first be apparent to firms in the same or related industries, so that they will be the first among potential purchasers.

To this extent, the operation of a rule banning horizontal merger might conflict with the efficient operation of the take-over constraint on managers, but this is not likely to be a serious problem. The existence of conglomerates guarantees that firms are prepared to acquire others in different industries. It is not necessary to risk monopoly to curb managerial discretion. Indeed, the operation of the rule could bring positive advantages insofar as it forced successful and efficient managers to look beyond their own industries for expansion opportunities. If there are unnecessarily sleepy backwaters in the economy, what better way to stir them up than by encouraging the entry of more energetic men than the firms' present managers?

---

[1] Robert Bork, 'Vertical Integration and the Sherman Act: The Legal History of an Economic Misconception', *University of Chicago Law Review*, 1954–1955, p. 197, provides a good economic analysis in addition to discussion of the application of US law. A more recent discussion is contained in W. S. Comanor, 'Vertical Mergers, Market Power and the Anti-Trust Laws', *American Economic Review*, May 1967, p. 254. J. S. McGee's comment on Comanor's paper, in the same issue, is also relevant.

VI. SUMMARY AND CONCLUSIONS

1. Is it possible to justify official intervention in business decisions which raise no conflict between public and private interests?—in which owners concerned to maximise their returns would take the same actions as a government concerned to allocate resources optimally? The only persuasive *rationale* seems to be that the interests of the owners of firms and of their managers conflict; that managers have substantial freedom to take decisions which run counter to those they would take were they themselves the owners; and that the results may be detrimental to others than the owners of firms. There would be little reason to pursue any other policy than one of *caveat emptor* in the purchase of shares were this last condition not fulfilled.

2. This rests on an empirical proposition, but the available evidence is too slight to support the case for official intervention. Nevertheless, the assertion that managers have substantial latitude cannot confidently be rejected on empirical grounds. The possibility that different managerial decisions would be better, both for the owners and the economy as a whole, remains open.

3. This is not to say that managerial decisions should be subject to official check. That would require a demonstration, not only of government competence, but also that the resources used in the checking procedure could not more profitably be employed elsewhere. Even a convincing demonstration that some feature of the private sector is less than perfect only makes a *prima facie* case for intervention by an omniscient government with infinite resources.

4. Supposing that there must be official action, is the best course a general surveillance, with officially administered rewards and penalties? The more generally undesirable features of such a programme are that it implies centralisation of decision-making and substantial discretionary power to its executive agencies. These characteristics might be acceptable were it shown that more efficiency in the use of resources would follow. But where will government find people competent to decide whether a particular decision is in the interests of the owners of a firm? There is no reason to expect that managerial decisions adverse for the public interest will occur in only one area. Even if, for

example, *all* merger decisions were rigorously examined, the heart of the problem would not have been reached. Why restrict the argument to merger? Why not all investment activity? Why not all decisions?[1]

5. The government does not now have the resources to undertake surveillance on such a broad front. It could, of course, employ experienced business men for that purpose. But then there is a question whether they would not better be employed in running their own firms. In any event, the justification for their employment is that salaried managers who receive bonuses for good performance cannot be relied upon to act in the interests of owners. Why assume that salaried managers who are employed by the state will act in the public interest? What incentive have they to do the hard thinking and take the unpleasant actions which would be necessary to exercise effective control over other decision-makers? The most that could be expected of such a procedure is that it would prevent grosser instances of inattention to the owners' interests and, by extension, to those of the public. But an effective market in corporate control could equally well be relied upon to serve this purpose.

6. People engaged in business *are* likely to be the most competent to judge whether another business could be run more profitably. That is the basis for the market in corporate control. If the managers of a firm are not making full use of the profitable opportunities available to them, or if their firm is for any reason valued at less than its potential, other managers will be the first to know it. For them such a firm is a profitable investment—a means of increasing their own incomes. It is unlikely that they will neglect the opportunity; it is even less likely if the market in corporate control is supplied with more information and if the capital costs of transactions within it are reduced.

[1] The former Secretary of State for Employment and Productivity apparently recognised the logic of this argument by her insistence that the proposed Commission for Industry and Manpower should have the power to investigate the affairs of any company with a capital of £10 million or more. (*Commission for Industry and Manpower Bill*, Bill 123, Part I, Clause 2, HMSO, 1970.) Logic could only take one to her position with the aid of an extreme and undemonstrated view of the powers of managers and the harm they may do. Since both the social losses from managerial latitude and the improvement to be expected from government investigation are uncertain, others might feel that if the logic of intervention dictates so large a degree of discretion, it could more impressively be used to argue against any such intervention.

7. But to restructure the institutions surrounding the market in corporate control might increase merger activity, and merger policy has been an area of debilitating indecision. The first page of *Mergers* asserts:

'. . . it would not be appropriate in Britain to formulate precise guide-lines to determine which mergers will be referred by the Board to the Commission; and though, as Chapters III and IV demonstrate, it is possible to list the aspects which are relevant for the public interest, it is not possible to settle in advance what weight should be attributed in a particular case to any particular aspect'.

Chapters III and IV list the 116 questions which the Board's merger panel 'may' ask. Most of them refer to issues which are best handled by other means—efficiency considerations, the balance of payments, regional policy, and redundancy—and merely reflect a lack of ability to distinguish what considerations are important for merger policy. What remain are the relevant issues for public policy: economies of scale and market power.

8. Annex 5 (1) of *Mergers* contains a speech by Mr Anthony Crosland, then President of the Board of Trade. In it, he gives two principal reasons for not specifying the conditions which will lead him to refer a merger to the Monopolies Commission. The first is that such guide-lines would imply that some types of market structure are undesirable in themselves, a position which would be inconsistent with the assumptions on which post-war monopoly legislation has been based. Secondly, the rules on mergers, '. . . while acceptable in a huge economy like the United States', are not in Britain:

'. . . in a smaller economy like ours, where necessary size may inevitably mean a certain degree of monopoly, such an approach could be very damaging in relation to international competition'.

The rule that concentration-increasing mergers should only be allowed to proceed subject to the demonstration of attainable economies of scale would conflict with neither of these requirements: it would simply make explicit and incorporate into a policy the reasons for not being dogmatic about industrial structure. It would thus remove the basis for much of the recent confusion and uncertainty in merger policy.

9. Nor is there good reason to suppose that measures of positive intervention—such as the establishment of the IRC—are necessary to ensure the efficient use of resources in the private sector. There is always a problem with official agencies given discretionary powers. If a body is established to promote mergers, for example, its members will look foolish if it does not do so. They have an incentive to appear active and vigorous even where action and vigour on their part are not appropriate from the economy's point of view. This is especially true, and likely to be a more serious problem, when a body can properly claim, as can the IRC, that the fruits of its labours will not appear in the immediate future. By the time they can be expected to appear, other events will have occurred to obscure interpretation of its consequences, and the harm, if any, will have been done. The establishment of such a body therefore requires particularly strong justification.

10. The case for the IRC, however, must be based either on the proposition that owners and managers are stupid and do not recognise their own interests, or that managers can act at considerable variance with the interests of the owners. The available evidence is indecisive on the last hypothesis and does not permit rejection of the *possibility* that some of the IRC's actions may eventually prove to have been in the public interest. But this must mean that there are institutional imperfections in the market for corporate control, and if that is so, public policy should be directed towards removing them. The IRC is a relatively small organisation—it cannot competently check the conduct of the entire private sector. Even if it were larger, there could be no strong argument against supplementing it with improved market action. But if the market can be improved why have the IRC?

11. Policies which substitute official action for market forces on the ground that managers cannot be relied upon to act in the interests of their owners are difficult to justify. They rely on the existence of institutional problems whose importance has not been well demonstrated, and they have appeared to proceed without inquiry into the possibility of correcting such imperfections as may exist. Much stronger rationalisations are required if official policy is to continue on its present course.

PROBLEMS

(Hobart Papers append questions to help teachers and students of economics to crystallise the author's analysis. Dr. Hindley has provided 'problems' for this purpose.)

I

Government officials frequently declare that large sections of British industry are managed inefficiently. It is possible to regard this proposition as wishful thinking: if British firms could obtain large increases in output without increasing their inputs, people living in Britain would be better off, and if that result could be achieved by exhortation or inspirational speeches, or even by a modest amount of tinkering, it would be rational to direct official energies in this direction rather than coming to grips with tougher problems. However, abstract from this factor. Suppose that a particular industry is identified as a victim of inefficient management. How would each of the following pieces of information affect your judgement on the appropriateness of the identification?

(1) The firms in the industry are owner-controlled. No new firm has attempted to enter the industry for several years.

(2) Ownership of the firms in the industry is widely dispersed. No firm has been subject to a take-over attempt.

(3) A take-over bidder took over one firm five years ago. The market share of that firm has increased substantially since then.

(4) The industry is dominated by one firm.

(5) Despite high tariff protection, imports of the industry's product have increased over the last few years.

(6) The industry has been losing its share of foreign markets. (Suppose it has been doing so at (a) the same rate as other export industries, (b) at a faster rate, (c) at a slower rate.)

(7) The same industry in the US consists of much larger

   (a) plants

   (b) firms.

(8) One firm in the industry has been expanding rapidly. Several others have gone bankrupt.

(9) The industry's executives contain a much lower proportion of university graduates than do most other industries.

(10) The industry has a much lower rate of return on capital than the average for all industries: its output has been contracting.

(11) One man in the industry has captured the public eye; however, with the present organisation of the industry, his firm is having trouble in increasing its market share.

(12) Firms in the industry spend little on research and development.

Discuss what other information might be useful to you in assessing the industry's efficiency. If the management of the firms in the industry were inefficient, what action would you wish to take? Would the form of this action depend upon the truth of any of the 'facts' cited above?

II

Industry X contains six firms, of which the largest has 35 per cent of the market, the smallest 5 per cent. Would the following merger proposals be against the public interest?

(1) The largest firm in the industry buys the smallest. (Would your view be affected by the information that the smallest firm had been growing more rapidly than its larger rivals?)

(2) The two smallest firms combine.

(3) The largest firm in the industry which supplies the X industry with its principal component (Y) buys the largest firm in X.

(4) The largest firm in Y buys the smallest firm in X.

(5) The smallest firm in X buys the largest firm in Y.

(6) A large firm from an entirely unrelated industry acquires the largest firm in X.

(7) The same as (6) but the large firm from an unrelated industry makes a take-over bid which is opposed by the incumbent managers. They threaten to quit if the bid succeeds.

Discuss what other information you might need (if any) to make up your mind.

FURTHER READING

Two excellent readings have not been referred to in this *Paper* because they did not come into my hands until after it was completed. They are *The Report of the White House Task Force on Anti-trust Policy* (the Neal Report); and *The Report of the Task Force on Productivity and Competition* (the Stigler Report). Both are reprinted in *The Journal of Reprints for Anti-trust Law and Economics* (Vol. I, Pt. I; Winter 1969). I would strongly recommend these Reports (and the various Dissents and Working papers appended).

Additional readings might include:

Manne, H. G., 'Mergers and the Market for Corporate Control', *Journal of Political Economy*, April 1965.

Tullock, Gordon, 'The New Theory of Corporations', in Erich Streissler (ed.), *Roads to Freedom*, Essays in Honour of F. A. von Hayek, Routledge & Kegan Paul, London, 1969.

The exchanges between Solow, Galbraith and Marris in *The Public Interest* (Fall 1967 and Spring 1968).

Alberts, W. W., and Segall, Joel E. (eds.), *The Corporate Merger*, University of Chicago Press, 1966.

Turner, Donald, 'Conglomerate Mergers and Section 7 of The Clayton Act', *Harvard Law Review*, May 1965.

Bork, Robert, 'Vertical Integration and the Sherman Act: The Legal History of an Economic Misconception', *University of Chicago Law Review*, 1954-55, p. 197.

Comanor, W. S., 'Vertical Mergers, Market Power and the Anti-Trust Laws', *American Economic Review*, May 1967, p. 254; also J. S. McGee's comment in the same issue.

Stigler, G. J., 'Monopoly and Oligopoly by Merger', *American Economic Review*, May 1950.

[It will be observed that these texts are American. Apart from studies of single industries it would seem there are no British general economic works on mergers. Dr Hindley's *Paper* should be doubly welcome to teachers and students of merger economics—ED.]